THE
COURAGE
TO
Hope

Christy-ana Williams-Rutil

NEWMAN SPRINGS PUBLISHING
320 Broad Street
Red Bank, NJ 07701

First originally published by Newman Springs Publishing 2022

ISBN 978-1-63692-296-6 (Paperback)
ISBN 978-1-63692-297-3 (Digital)

Printed in the United States of America

Dear Daddy,
are you coming home?

For every little girl who has lost a parent

PROLOGUE

Losing a parent is one of the most difficult things that any child has to face. Sometimes it is extremely more painful when the loss is not because the person died but the person has made a choice not to be with you. Sometimes you still wonder why that person who is still alive does not want to be a part of your life. Sometimes you wonder, "Did I do something wrong to cause the loss?" When you think about why the person, especially a parent, does not want to be in your life, it sometimes can cause stress, suicide, and even hatred. But with Jesus, you can feel whole again. Let's think about it: it's their choice whether they want to be with you or not. Just remember, you are unique, you are special, and you are a very important gem; and if someone does not appreciate you enough to want to be with you, then it is their loss. This took me a really long time to understand. The pain that I felt that day I was separated from my daddy and the pain that followed years and years to come was unimaginable. But if you hope in the Lord's unfailing love, He can help you because it helped me to depend on my Heavenly Father. My Heavenly Daddy gave me everything that my earthly father could not give me—PEACE. Thank You, Lord.

He heals the brokenhearted
and binds up their wounds.

—Psalm 147:3

August 18, 2014

Dear Daddy,

    I can still remember the look on your face and see the tears in your eyes that day my mom and I boarded the plane back to Boston. We waved each other for a long time until the plane disappeared into the trees. I was so sad, and my mom kept saying that you would be back home in Boston soon. But I did not care about that. All I wanted was my daddy—the one who made silly faces at me and tricked me when he wanted to leave the house to go to the store. I wanted to hear his voice, hear him say, "Christy, look. 'Dada,'" and I would fly into his arms. I just wanted my daddy. I cried all the way to Boston. I cried the day after and many months and then years to come. I did not care what my mommy said; all I wanted was to see my daddy.

    It was September, and there I was again crying in my classroom because you still did not come home. How sad I felt when my friend's dad came to pick them up from school, wishing it was my daddy. What will I do without my teacher; she sure knew exactly how to make me feel better when I cried for my daddy. Although my mommy knew the right words to say to make me feel better, it still did not minimize my pain.

    It has been a couple years, and my daddy still has not come home to stay permanently. I do not know if he ever will, but my hope lies in the Lord. He keeps telling me next month and next month, which never comes. I keep hoping and hoping and praying. I keep praying and praying, but I feel all my hopes are gone. "Pray for him," my mom would say. Yes! I prayed and believed that God would answer my prayers. Daddy, I am still waiting for you.

I love you, Daddy,
Chae

Consider it pure joy, my brothers and sisters, whenever
you face trials of many kinds, because you know that
the testing of your faith produces perseverance.

—James 1:2–3

September 18, 2014

Dear Daddy,

It has been many years; and you still keep going back and forth, missing my birthdays, Thanksgivings, and Christmas. Holidays suck because I do not have a daddy to spend it with. My mom tries to make it fun, but it is never the same without my daddy. Usually we go to my grandma's house and then my aunt's house to spend Thanksgiving. I think that's my mom's way of making sure we are not alone. I am supposed to feel better, but I do not. I see my uncle with his kids playing around, and remembering I have no daddy to play with makes me feel worse. I just want to go home, close my bedroom door, and sleep until Thanksgiving is over.

The next day is a new day. Though you are still not home, the holiday stress is over; and I can do what I usually do—listen to music, draw, pray with my mommy, and go to the park. Thank God the holiday stress is over. Just me and my mommy doing stuff. Sometimes it is boring, but sometimes it is fun. My dad's family thinks that I am okay. They always say how such a great mom my mommy is, but what do they know? Every little girl needs her daddy. It is horrific for little girls who do not have their daddy. I felt so safe and happy when Daddy was here; now I have to pretend to be happy because everyone thinks I am so perfect.

Love,
Chae

For I know the plans I have for you, declares the LORD, plans for welfare and not for evil, to give you a future and a hope.

—Jeremiah 29:11

December 25, 2014

Dear Dad,

It is Christmas, and you are still not home. But I get to spend Christmas with my grandparents and cousins in Saint Thomas. Christmas was amazing—both my grandmas make the best oatmeal ever. Saint Thomas is beautiful, and the food is priceless. Aunty Rowina do cook some of the best meals, and they are vegetarians. Whoever thought vegetarian food could be so tasty. Truthfully, I had the best Christmas since Daddy was gone.

I love you, Daddy,
Chae

The pain that you've been feeling, can't compare to the joy that's coming.

—Romans 8:18

January 18, 2015

Dearest Daddy,

When are you coming? It has been months we last saw you. Are you okay? Are you thinking of me as I am of you? What could be keeping you away from me for so long? Mommy said I should not worry, pray. I want to be brave and strong. I want to believe that God can answer all prayers, but I am losing faith. The more I pray, the sadder I feel because it is as if God is not hearing my prayers. Doesn't God know that a little girl needs her daddy? Why is he allowing me to wait for so long?

I wish you were here, Daddy. I told Mom last night that we should visit you in Dominica or move there. I hate not having you at home. I had a family, and now I have no family. A mom alone is not a family. Daddy, you messed up my perfect family. I want to believe that you still love me and you did not leave because of me, but that's all I think about. You were always here before I was born; now I am here, especially now, you choose to go to Dominica. This is really sad. What do I have to do to show you how much we miss you and want you to come home?

My mom pretends that she is tough and is not missing you, but I can hear her crying in the bathroom at nights and see her sadness all the time. I know she misses you too. Sometimes I wonder if mom did something to drive you away, but she would not do that. She loves me more than herself and would do practically anything to make me happy. So I know she did not cause you to leave. Do you think it is wise for a man to leave his family and just disappear? I know that God did not ordain that move, but I am confident that God will not take you permanently away from me. So I have hope.

Sincerely,
Chae

Rejoice in hope, be patient in tribulation, be constant in prayer.

—Romans 12:2

March 18, 2015

Dearest Daddy,

You have no idea how happy I was when you surprised me in school. That was one of the happiest days of my life. There I was in school thinking about you, and there you were. Was it a coincidence, or are we connected by some powerful force? My mom always say that I can smell my daddy in another country. I do believe her. I always felt your presence when you were coming home. Even if I was sleeping, I would wake up when I thought you were there, and luckily you were pulling your car in the driveway.

Being so close to you has brought so much pain to me you cannot imagine. I know you believe that you are not hurting me by being away, but you are wrong. You are destroying me. Sometimes I feel I should not pray anymore because God does not answer my prayers. How could a God so amazing to me make me suffer so much for you? Now I understand my brother's pain.

I believe you do not know better because you are not a Christian. When you are in the world and do not know God, all you do is wrong things, which includes hurting your loved ones. I am praying for God to reveal Himself to you so you can see how much you are hurting me. I love you, Daddy, and I am praying for you every day. Even if there are times I get discouraged and feel hopeless, I believe in God when He says He will take care of me.

I will always love you, Daddy,
Chae

When you go through deep waters, I will be with you.

—Isaiah 43:2

July 18, 2015

Dearest Daddy,

Today was another happy day of my life because you are home. My mom completely tricked me. She said she was going to the airport to get my auntie who was coming to visit us. I was so happy that I was going to see my auntie. We got dressed around six o'clock and headed for the airport. Traffic was horrendous as could be expected; we were going during rush hour. Going to the airport when workers are on their way home would take triple times what it would usually take, so it took us a little longer maneuvering traffic to get there.

On our arrival to the airport, I was sound asleep, so tired from the long day we had at school. All I can remember is my mom stopping the car. I do not know how it happened, but I knew that I smelled my daddy. I was not sure if subconsciously I was hoping he was there or I was just wishing that he would come off the plane. I remember I leaped out of the car as she stopped at the airport and ran into your arms. My mom is still shocked by what occurred. She is still baffled by how quickly I got up and ran straight into my daddy's arms. She is still wondering if I knew you were coming, imagined, or dreamed about it during my trip to the airport or it was just that connection we have. Either way, it was amazing to see you.

I had so much fun when you came, but the truth is that excitement was quickly relinquished when you left again. I wonder if my life is ever going to be happy again. Though I am excited when you come, I become more depressed soon after because I know that you will be leaving soon. And as predicted, you left again for another three, maybe six months—who knows.

I wish you all the best, Daddy.

Love,
Chae

But if we hope for what we do not see,
we wait for it with patience.

—Romans 8:25

July 24, 2015

Dearest Daddy,

What I missed most about you not being at home is your fun. When you left, it's like a light went out inside of me. I kept trying to rekindle that fire, but it is as if it is gone forever. You brought light into my life, and now you are not here, the light has finally disappeared. Sometimes I wonder, Will I ever be happy again? How can you be happy when your source of happiness is destroyed?

I love my mommy, and she makes me happy. But it is just not the same without you. Sometimes I try to wonder why God allows people to go through pain and hardship. It feels like it is simple. He can just end all pain; He is God and has all power. Then again, as my mom says, "Do not question God." Well! I try not to, but who else can I question? My mom still does not know why you left, and you cannot give a truthful answer. So all I can do is speculate. You guys were happy and together before I was born; did I break you up?

Bye, Daddy.

She is clothed in strength, and dignity, and
she laughs without fear of the future.

—Proverbs 31:25

September 18, 2016

Dear Dad,

I just wanted to take this opportunity to say thank you for your love throughout my younger years. I am the child that I am today because of you and Mom, though mostly my mom—no offense. You taught me the value of being persistent and the importance of following your dreams. But I never would have become a successful preacher and an A student if it weren't for my mom, who cried with me practically every night for many, many years. I should love to say you are my rock, that you were there for me, but the truth is my mom was also my daddy.

However, I do thank you for the very valuable lesson you have taught me. Through your actions, I have learned that I can only depend on Jesus. I cannot depend on you for the simplest life skills to the more complicated ones, such as how to stand up after facing failure, but I can depend on Jesus. These are lessons I will keep with me for the rest of my life.

I love you with all my heart, Daddy. But if it was not for Jesus and my mom, you could have destroyed me forever.

Love,
Your little girl

Be bold. Be brave. Be courageous.

—Joshua 1:9

October 18, 2017—California

Dear Dad

Because I have a father like Jesus, I can hold my head up high. I'm proud to say that my Father is a man of strength and kindness when I think about what He went through for me. I wish one day you can emulate some of His selfless character. Though you have brought a lot of pain in my life, I still believe that you have some really great qualities that others can copy. You have taught me so much in life unintentionally—like how to stand up when I fall. Because every time you left me, I felt like I would fall; and with Jesus, I had to muster the courage to get up. My only wish for you is to take these lessons and do something with your life that Jesus would be proud of.

As I get older, I miss you less; and now it seems that if you do not come up, it is not a big deal because I always expect disappointments from you. However, I always carry you with me in my heart. But Jesus is in my soul, and that makes such a difference. He is the guiding force in my life, and I would be lost without Him. I am praying for you, Daddy.

Chae

There is a time for everything and a reason
for every activity under the heavens.

—Ecclesiastes 3:1

November 18, 2017

Dear Dad,

    I remember when I was a little girl, I would sit on your shoulders and feel so tall. As I got older, I learned that you were only human and that you too could make mistakes. But now that I am a teenager, I have learned that you are the balance between invincibility and vulnerability. You are proud, strong, and capable. But you are also vulnerable when you need to be. Now that I am older, I just want you to know that you can be anything you want to be, and I will still be the faithful daughter who will be by your side.

Love you, Daddy.

Don't be afraid, for I am with you. Don't be discouraged,
for I am your God. I will strengthen you and help you.
I will hold you up with my victorious right hand.

—Isaiah 41:10

December 18, 2017

Dear Dad.

    I do believe that one day, we will be together again.

    I believe that you will be the super hero of my childhood again. I have faith that you will come back home to me, so whenever there is something I wanted to know, I can count on you to teach me. Whenever I feel scared because my mom and I are alone, scared that someone can break into our house and hurt us, I believe that you'd be there to scare them off with your booming voice. I want you to be there whenever boys try to break my young heart. You, not my mom, will comfort me and ask me if I want you to deal with the boy. Dad, you are and will always be my superhero, and I will forever be your little princess. So please come home.

Chae

"I will not cause pain without allowing something new to be born," says the Lord.

—Isaiah 66:9

January 18, 2018

Dear Dad,

You are the number one person in my life who has really taught me the true value of forgiveness. I remember when I would scream at my mom because she wouldn't let me get my way, she would scold me, and you just stood there and watch it happen without saying a word. Sometimes I hoped you would come and rescue me. As I got older, I later learned that this was you teaching me that I won't always get what I want in the world.

I remember when I said things to Mommy, you would say, "Don't say that, Christy," but smile and love me anyway. This taught me that a parent can never truly be angry at their child no matter how awful they've been. I believe you love me daddy, but why are you hurting me? If you love me so much as you claim, can you please put my needs above your own? Right now, I need you, and you are not there.

Remember when you say, "Christy, I am coming up," but you never do. This shows that you do not care if I hurt or not. Daddy, I am hoping that you allow Jesus to change your life so you can make it to the kingdom. Life is not just about making yourself happy but also about making Jesus and others happy too.

I am praying for you, Daddy,
Chae

But I will hope continually, and will yet
praise thee more and more.

—Psalm 71:14

February 18, 2018

Dear Daddy,

    I remember when I would cry my eyes out and think that my life is ruined because you weren't there, my mom would hold me in her arms and tell me that everything is going to be okay. This taught me that a mother will do anything to make her daughter okay again. Mommies truly are miracle workers. However, I wish it was you here holding me, convincing me that everything will be okay.

    But I thank God I have a daddy. I have friends and cousins who do not have a daddy.

I am praying for you,
Chae

Do not grieve, for the joy of the Lord is your strength.

—Nehemiah 8:10

March 18, 2018

Dear Daddy,

I write to you not only as your daughter but as one of many daughters who understand the distinctive complexities of the lessons only fathers could teach. I write to you because out of every guidance I have received, from you—though limited—are more profound than any other. It is because yours is solely based on protection and strength. Not that mommy's was not, but hers is more based on emotions and faith. The few times that you were present, you've always stood back and allow me to sparkle, only stepping in when I call for you. But knowing that you are far away, sometimes I call, and you cannot come to me. So I drown myself in tears.

Daddy! You can be an amazing, I have some experience of that. I have seen you do remarkable things—buying mommy flowers, returning your best sneakers so I could get the expensive one that I wanted, and giving to the poor and needy. Please do not allow the darkness of Lucifer to dim your true light. It's time I use these words to yank you and every other incredible father into the light you so deserve to be seen in. It's time that light exudes on the genuine and astonishing love that only a daddy can show his daughter.

A father's job entails teaching his daughter several lessons about what it means to truly love and encounter this life. One of the most crucial understandings he can show to the eager young eyes looking up at him is the idea of how she should be treated. Daddy, I remember everything. I remember being tucked in at night and kissed goodbye before you left for the store and waiting up all night until you return. I remember every time my mom begs you to wear a suit, how unhappy you were but you wore it anyway to make us happy. I remember having you carry my doll around the mall for hours when we went shopping and how silly you looked, now as I thought about it, but you would do anything to make me happy, even if it meant you were unhappy or looked ridiculous. Where has all those feelings gone?

I remember every chocolate sundae and long talk shared on drives home from the trips we took. I remember every time you selflessly did what I wanted because you wanted to make me happy. I remember every time you exhibit awe-inspiring patience and grace when I cried because I needed your attention. I remember it all because it lives in the heart of a daughter forever. Daddy! I want to make more memories with you, but I cannot if you are not here.

Most times, a reliable and trustworthy father figure can become a scarcity today. There are so many children without a daddy, and sadly the fathers are not dead. They are still alive. I am not saying you have not been a great dad, but you have not always been there. Now you have the choice to change that. You have to decide what you want. You are alive and well and missing out on so many things in my life. I'm not saying that I am not happy that you are alive; all I am saying is I want you to be in my life. I feel blessed enough to be graced with one like you, but there is so much you can be. You can be the father and husband God created you to be. We watched the way you whip up a great salad or fruit bowl for movie night. I wish I had movie nights every Saturday night and not just every couple months. These are the images that inscribe themselves in my young and impressionable heart as I grow into a young woman.

Remember, we learn to love the way we were loved. So if you gave me crappy love, it is a high possibility that you have messed me up for life. But thank God for His amazing grace. I know everyone has very high expectations of me because my parents set the bar high. I have had high hopes for myself because Christ has taught me that love from another should be respectful, honest, and encouraging. As a father, you taught me some great things, and you were barely there. Can you imagine how much more I could learn if you are actually here? You are not just preparing me for today but for the distant future man that may want to come into my life.

Fathers are the first male daughters will love. Dad, you held me, played with me, and supported me consistently for only a couple years of my life. For the rest of my life, you were hardly there, and it is time you put my needs above yours. I know deep within you lies my amazing daddy. You believed in me first. You held me first. You gave me all I could have ever needed until that day when you were taken out of my life. I refuse to believe that you just left me after loving me so dearly, so I imagine that the devil took you from me. I am praying you back home, and I will not stop praying because God answers prayer. Because I know you love me, you will find your way back to me. You showed me that love is being strong and humble, so I am patiently awaiting you because I love you.

I know that one day you'll be the dad you were supposed to be. Daddy, I want you to know that I will never let you go. I know that you have not been there for me, but I will chase you. The Bible says, "Ye who he loves he chastened." Though I encounter much pain because you are not here, I dream that one day you will be with me. I choose to believe that even when you are not here, you are still back there watching me and waiting for my call. I know that in my heart, there is no love like the first love, and that part of me will always belong to my daddy.

Forever,
Chae

He will cover you with His feathers, and under His wings, you will find refuge; His faithfulness will be your shield and rampart.

—Psalm 91:4

July 18, 2018

Dear Dad.

Today I am preaching to hundreds of people, and I wish you were one of them. Preaching is a talent God gave me, and I wish you could help me share Jesus. Daddy! You have not been all I know you can be, and you are not doing a great job as a daddy. Please don't be sad. I know that I've always been your little girl. I was your baby, the helpless little one whom you always had to take care of at one, two, and three years old. My tears came easy, but your love and guidance came easier.

Daddy, you should know that I would be sad because you are no longer with me. Daddy, I want you to know that you are the reason I am always sad and stressed. Sometimes I feel you do not know the job of a real daddy. You showed me how to love, and then now you are showing me that love is transient. You have not been a good example of what it means to be a father and a husband to Mommy. And it's because of you that I sometimes feel I am not good enough.

I wish I could say thank you, Dad, for laying the foundations for me and showing me what I need in this life, but only Mommy gets that credit. Parenting is not just a mother's job; it is yours too.

I am still praying for you,
Chae

My soul finds rest in God alone, my salvation comes
from Him, He alone is my rock and my salvation.

—Psalm 62:1–2

August 18, 2018

Dear Daddy,

It is another birthday, and I am sad because you did not even call me. All I have is memories. I still remember those precious times when you would carry me on your shoulders so that I could see the splendor of the world, carry me when I pretended to be asleep so that I did not have to walk. It was then I was convinced that God knew what He was doing when He chose you to be my dad. You were always the calm, tender presence who would direct me. You would speak up and say what needed to be said without yelling or hesitation. I see that even though you weren't as hands on as Mom, your presence showed me that you would always be there for me. Now if I fail, you are not there to help me up.

Daddy, I want you to be here with me. What changed, Daddy? Don't you love me anymore? I thank God I have Him as a daddy and I can carry Him in my heart always. He is forever present in my life, and whenever I need him, He runs to me. He does not say, "I have to do this, Christy," or "I have to do that, Christy." He drops whatever He is doing and runs to me. You should make Christ your example. God is not done with you yet, Daddy.

Your little girl,
Chae

I can do everything through Christ who gives me strength.

—Philippians 4:13

September 18, 2018

Dear Dad,

While Mom taught me how to talk, to walk, to count, and to read, you instructed me on one of the most essential things I needed in life—how to laugh. Daddy, you are so funny. You showed me that there is hilarity and joy all over the world, and all it takes to see it is a little budge in your perception. People might condemn you for being too carefree with everything, but I could see what you were doing— you just wanted me to be happy.

Mommy had her role; you had yours. Now you are gone, how do you think I feel? You always dealt with things in a way that made huge problems less stressful. A little laughter here and a smirk there could encourage even the most dispirited person to pull through and succeed. I need this spark in my life daddy, but I think you have forgotten how to smile. In times when my life was dark and apparently worthless, I would remember the jolly face of my father and march on with a joy in my heart. You truly lit up my life, Dad, and now you are gone. I feel the pang of darkness at times. But God in His mercy gives me peace.

I love you.

For I know the plans I have for you, plans to prosper you
and not harm you, plans to give you hope and a future.

—Jeremiah 29:11

November 18, 2018

Dear Daddy,

I would often hear people tell stories about their anxieties as parents. Many parents today seem so scared of the world that they want to guard their children from it. Dad, that is how you and Mommy raised me. At first, I thought you cared too much if I saw the unfriendliness in the world. Then I thought you were being a robust dad who didn't care if I cried or got terrified. Others would say it is tough love. However, I later realized that this was your way of showing me the actuality of this world.

You sheltered me from instant danger, but you never shy away from disclosing how treacherous this world can be. Many think that this is a definite way to craft a frightened child, but with Mom's guidance and your love, you all have made me a stronger child. I want you to continue helping me to build, Daddy, but you are not here. How can I face the giants in my life without you? I know that I will be a self-reliant woman one day who may want to take on the world on her own, but I still need you here to help me take it on. However, I know that if you choose not to show up, God will show up for me. From a very early age, you taught me how to be brave and audacious. Thanks for the tough love, Dad! Now I need that tough love even more.

Love you,
Chae

So do not fear, for I am with you; do not be dismayed,
for I am your God. I will strengthen you and help you;
I will uphold you with my righteous right hand.

—Isaiah 41:10

December 18, 2018

Dear Daddy,

I just wanted to thank you for everything you have ever done for me even though it was just a little and Mommy did all the work. Moms are heroes. They do things that usually dads are expected to do like fixing things in my room when it is broken, showing me how to ride a bike, teaching me how to recognize a truthful and a dishonest boy, paying my school fees for ten years, picking me up and dropping me off to school, and taking out the trash. And this is just the daddy's role; it doesn't even scratch the surface of the mommy's role. I can only imagine how difficult it was for her being in the role of both father and mother at the same time, but she made it seem like the coolest thing ever and the most natural thing in the world. She showed me what a real mother would do for her little girl.

I wish you were still here, Daddy, to do things with me—manly things. My mom made me see that even though it was just her and me, there was nothing missing in my life. She fulfilled every task you needed to fulfill—from being my pillar of strength to my motivation. You missed out on so many things in my life, Daddy, but I forgive you; and I am giving you another chance because I love you. You were the most awesome dad a daughter could ever wish for, and you allow the devil to take over you. Fight him, Daddy. Find Jesus and fight him.

I am praying for you,
Chae

The Lord is my strength and my song; he has given me victory.

—Exodus 15:2

January 18, 2019

Dear Daddy,

I can vaguely remember when I was a little girl and you would go out of the house either to work or the supermarket. I would stay up all night praying for you to come back quickly until I would finally fall asleep. I remember how I would practically force you to play the same game over and over again and then put on my puppy face when you wanted to quit because we were playing for such a long time. And you would just let me have fun because you did not want me to feel sad. I'm sure there were times you were at your wit's end, but you never show it.

I miss having fun with you, Daddy. You were such a great daddy. I remember how you would always look so worried when I'd go off to school or go to play with the neighbors and you would insist that my mom had to be outside with me. I understand now why you guys were so protective of me. I guess what I'm trying to say is that now that I'm older and I see on the news how mean and hurtful people can be, I am learning to trust even more what my parents says because they know what is best for me. I just wish you were here to help Mommy raise me.

I am praying for you.

Love you, Daddy,
Chae

So do not fear, for I am with you; do not be dismayed,
for I am your God. I will strengthen you and help you;
I will uphold you with my righteous right hand.

—Isaiah 41:10

February 18, 2019

To my excitable, flippant, diplomatic, and obsessively organized dad,

This is your daughter trying to make fun of you for a change. You've always been such a hilarious person—a laugh from you was something to be admired. People think you're way too serious even when you're around kids, but people do not know you like me. You are a fun daddy. Playtimes would often be full of joy especially playing Scrabble when I beat you, and you always thought I was being dishonest. But I was not; it is because I am way smarter than you.

As a kid, I did not quite understand the meaning of your parenting style. I just thought you just love to have fun. Mommy gets too serious at times. I miss having fun with you. It is all about reading for Mommy. Please come back to me, Daddy. I did not realize how amazing you truly were. Now that you are gone, I keep telling myself I wish I could get a daddy do-over, and I will hold you so close and never let you go. As I get older, I realize the value of cherishing your family, and it pains my heart that my family may never be the same again and that my daddy is gone forever. But my faith in God will keep going until Jesus decides that it is time for me to let go. Even though you are hardly with me in Boston, the few years you spent with me in the early years of my life was awesome, and I thank God that I had that time with you.

The way you took care of me and protected me showed just how much you loved me. Your hugs, kisses, and words of love always made me feel immaculate. There was never a day when we didn't have our fruit/vegetable bowls at dinner. And while you weren't a huge fan of going to church, you were always listening for hours when I preach to you on Sunday mornings before breakfast. Even when you got tired and hungry, you sat there and listened; and you always clapped at the end and said, "Good job, Christy. You are the best." You always told me to pray before I eat. Daddy, I just love when you put me to bed because I would convince you to play with me late especially when Mommy is at a meeting. I remember when she would get home and complain about me being up so late and your favorite line, "Leave the child alone."

Dad, I know deep down inside, you are still there. I need you to reach deep within yourself and pull my daddy out. Nothing is impossible for God to do. So the same God who raised Lazarus from the dead and made a blind man see is the same God who is going to bring you back to me. I believe that. I forgive you for hurting me, Daddy, because I know you did not leave me on your own; it was orchestrated by the devil. Trust in God, and He will do amazing things in your life. I still believe that you have the power over sin.

I love you, Daddy,
Chae

So do not fear, for I am with you;

do not be dismayed, for I am your God.
I will strengthen you and help you;
I will uphold you with my righteous right hand.

—Isaiah 41:10

March 18, 2019

Dad,

When I sit back and ponder on all the innumerable times that you carried me on your shoulders, I am assured that the God whom I serve knew what He was doing when He chose you to be my dad. The man that inspired me to reach for the stars was you. I am thankful for all the things you prepared me for the perils of life—the hurt and pain I may encounter. Though you are not in my life right now, I still remember those valuable lessons.

Although you were never as vociferous as Mommy and never picked up a book to read with me, your impact and your calm yet resilient attitude was always there, and these are some qualities that still tower over me. I have now truly realized the true depth and breadth of your presence throughout my life. Those memories were so short-lived. Let's make more memories together, Daddy.

You are always loved!
Your girl

But those who hope in the Lord
will renew their strength.
They will soar on wings like eagles;
they will run and not grow weary,
they will walk and not be faint.

—Isaiah 40:31

April 18, 2019

Dear Daddy,

I know you to be always affectionate and nurturing, to be warmhearted and soft, and to be attentive and kindhearted. What happened to you? Now it appears that you show no care for me. You barely call me, and you are always busy. I am what that matters, Daddy; nothing that you are doing is more important than me. I am what matters. Jesus first and then my needs. Check your priority, Daddy. Remember you are not always going to be young, and just how I need you today, you will need me tomorrow. You being this way makes me wonder about your relationship with God. That's why I am praying for you, Daddy. There are no words to describe my immeasurable love for you. But I need you to step up and be the daddy God created you to be.

When I was growing up, I know that you put my needs ahead of yours, but now I doubt that is the truth. Your behavior has caused me incalculable agony. Your way of dealing with things has become too carefree, and I just wish you would take our relationship more seriously and do something. I am praying for you, but you need to pray too. Praying without ceasing should be your daily agenda because the devil has tied you down; he has put a wool over your eyes so you cannot see me. Pray that He removes the wool so you can see my beautiful face—the same baby girl you fell in love with on August 18, 2006. Please, my Daddy. Let God be your tower of strength.

Your daughter,
Chae

My flesh and my heart may fail,
but God is the strength of my heart
and my portion forever.

—Psalm 73:26

May 18, 2019

Dear Daddy,

I hope you know how blessed I feel to have you in my life even if I see you only couple of months. I just wish you would be with me forever because I love you so much! I'm super proud to be your daughter because you are such a determined dad. No words penned on paper can accurately articulate the love I feel for you. Whenever you picked me up me in your strapping, comfortable arms and swathed me in the warmest and skintight hug imaginable, I knew you were the man that would always be my safe haven.

Whenever you either drop me off to school or pick me up, you made me so happy. I always wanted you to drop me off to school or pick me up because I wanted to show you off to my teachers and friends because I love you so much and I was so proud of you, Daddy. Now I do not know if I even want you to pick me up from school because I am so disappointed in you. You just left me and do not care how I feel. Why is it that parents just leave and think they are hurting the other parent when the child is the one they are hurting the most? Daddy, I want you to know that you did not just leave Mommy when you left us; you hurt me too. Every school year, I anticipate that this is the year that I will get my daddy back, but the years trudge on and no Daddy.

Thanks for being the best you can be without Jesus—but no thanks for walking away.

I love you!
Chae

That is why, for Christ's sake, I delight in weaknesses,
in insults, in hardships, in persecutions, in difficulties.
For when I am weak, then I am strong.

—2 Corinthians 12:10

June 18, 2019

Dear Dad,

I am really and exceedingly blessed to have you as my daddy. You are my greatest supporter, my very best bud, my pillar, and my encouragement. Dad, when you tell me that I can do something, I believe and feel completely invincible. I am losing my invincibility since you're gone. Mommy tries to take your place, but she is not good at it. I used to always be able to count on you in every horrid situation I find myself in. There is absolutely no doubt that God took a slice of you to create me for the person I am—a tinier, girlier form of my daddy.

Your unrelenting confidence in my illimitable potential emboldens me each day. I can't thank God enough for having you in my life, so that's why I'm praying that I do not lose you, Daddy. I am praying that you will come to God and He will work in you so that you can be a vessel for Him and also be a real daddy again. Daddy, I will always be the best gift you got from life, and you will also be my best gift, packaged with Jesus.

You always say that life will not be a "bed of roses," and you are correct it is not. But with you in my life, I believe though trials come, you can give me the strength. Though Jesus is my strength, a little girl still needs her daddy to help her gain that mental strength. For now my Heavenly Daddy is looking over me, but I still need my earthly daddy.

I love you, Daddy,
Chae

I love you, Lord, my strength.
The Lord is my rock, my fortress and my deliverer;
my God is my rock, in whom I take refuge,
my shield and the horn of my salvation, my stronghold.

—Psalm 18:1–2

June 18, 2019

Dear Dad,

From traveling all over the US and reading several novels to playing basketball and drawing stick figures, there hasn't been a single moment in my life where your words of wisdom and guidance hasn't helped to shape me into who I am. I have countless father-daughter memories from the earlier years of my life I can cherish, but I need some new memories as a teenager to last me a lifetime. Though I am thankful for all memories I have of us, I need more. Every moment that we have ever spent together is an extraordinary experience. All those memories are thickly embedded within my heart.

There are endless reasons why you can be the greatest dad in the world for your little girl. You are very endorsing of my every ambition and assisting me get through them. I have my whole life ahead of me, and I still need you in my corner. Remember, you always trained me to never quit even when life is difficult. I promise I won't ever give up on you and I won't quit praying for you.

Behind every great daughter is truly an exceptionally amazing father like you, so when people say how amazing I am, I think of you. It is not too late to turn around and run back to me, Daddy.

Loads of love, Daddy!
Love you to the moon and back, Dada!
Your wonderful daughter

But I will sing of your strength,
in the morning I will sing of your love;
for you are my fortress,
my refuge in times of trouble.

—Psalm 59:16

July 18, 2019

Dear Daddy,

I know that you always tend to display a robust, impassive exterior, and I understand that it is to conceal your weakness for me. Every time I ask for something in the past, you always try to be firm, but you cannot because you love me too much. I have gotten to that age now, and I can see your intentions clearly after everything you have ever done for me. They were all done through love. It is only because you wanted me to always have what I need and wanted and never feel less. I can now judge what you have done for me was a manifestation of true love. I miss that attention, Daddy. I am now at the age when I need more of that attention, and you are not there to give it to me. Please come home, Daddy. I miss you.

I would like to shout it over the hilltop that I surely have been gifted with the most amazing dad in the world. I just want you to know that and be there for me. When God created me, He knew that I would need a daddy just like you, and I know He did not create you just to give up on me. He did not give me you just to take you away from me. That is not how my amazing Father in heaven works. So I know that you will be back. I just need to ask the Lord for loads of patience, much strength, and the power to pray because Christ has assured us no good deed will He hold from us.

You have been the throttlehold in my life for a long time, and it appears that you are slipping away. Please allow Jesus to hold on to you. When you feel weak, He will give you the strength. Make Jesus your firm foundation and build your life on Him. I need you, Daddy. I need to you to always encourage and motivate me like you used to when I was younger. I need you to escort me through the ups and downs and my excursion of life. I know you will be there; I am counting on it.

Love you!

For the word of God is alive and active. Sharper than any double-edged sword, it penetrates even to dividing soul and spirit, joints and marrow; it judges the thoughts and attitudes of the heart.

—Hebrews 4:12

August 18, 2019

Dearest Daddy,

I will always love you for the assistance, security, and inspiration I got from you. Although many may disagree, to me, you were the most awesome daddy ever; and I cannot say so now. I wish I could. But the fact is you are never there, and that hurts me more than you can ever know. More than that, you were my playfellow, superman, trainer, and guide; and now that you are not there, it is difficult for me. The world sees an amazing little girl, but what they do not see is the little girl who cries herself to sleep every night because she misses her daddy. You always taught me to have faith and believe that God can do the impossible.

I have faith that He will bring you back to me. Truthfully, sometimes I lose faith; but I thank God that when I am weak, He makes me strong. I thank God that in my weakness, he gives me strength. Daddy, you showed me to become the stout young lady I am today. Daddy, there are no words to describe the unceasing love and unwavering support you have showered me within my younger years. I am still craving for more. Please come home.

When I glance back at all the wonderful moments we have shared, I constantly have to hold the tears back. I know that my life was perfect with you in it; now it is not at all what the Lord had in mind for me. However, I still will not replace you. I am trying harder every day to love more and appreciate more and to emulate Christ.

Love you more than anything!
Chae

Though my father and mother forsake
me, the LORD will receive me.

—Psalm 27:10

September 18, 2019

Dear Daddy,

I wrote this story in my class. Sometimes I wonder, Am I the lonely tree waiting for my daddy to find me?

The Lonely Tree

There it stood in the green meadow, in the back of an abandoned house for ages, wondering if someone noticed it's there. Birds flew by, ants and snakes crawled under, and squirrels climbed onto it—none realizing it was lonely or stopping to say hi. This tree was waiting for someone to trim its leaves or put water in his roots, but nobody did. This tree cried every single night waiting in anticipation for someone to come and love him and take care of him. Sometimes he would just wish that someone could come and cut him down. But that one day, a girl found him.

It was a sunny morning. Emily and her father were looking to buy a house. They didn't want an ugly house, but they wanted a cheap house. So they drove and drove until they came across the main road in the exact same place where the tree is located.

So Emily put her head outside the car window and said, "Daddy! Daddy! Look at this house. It's for sale."

Then Emily's father said, "Good job, Emily. Good looking."

Emily's dad stopped the car to look at the number on the sign for sale post and then called it. They asked the lady if they can take a look at the house just to see if that's what they needed. The lady said she will be there in ten minutes. So Emily and her father decided to go to Burger King and eat as they waited.

Emily and her father finished eating and headed back to the house. As soon as they arrived, Emily jumped out the car with excitement, ready to get a tour. Emily loves getting tours especially house tours. So Emily and her father walked inside. Even though this house was abandoned and ugly from the outside, it was pretty inside. Emily and her father's reaction was priceless. They loved it so much all they said was wow, wow, and wow! The lady that was giving them a tour said to go outside and see how beautiful it is. When Emily reached outside, the first thing she noticed was how big that tree was. It's so beautiful; it just needs to get trim and watered.

Emily's dad said, "We can get the house, but we have to cut down the tree because it is hovering over the pool."

Emily didn't care about the pool; she just wanted to take care of the tree and make it grow bigger than what it was already. So she climbed up the tree and gave a hug and told it a secret.

She said, "I will never let no one cut you down."

The tree felt so happy that someone noticed him and loved him, so he told the girl, "Thank you."

Although Emily was surprised that the tree spoke to her, she was not scared or frightened, just shocked.

"You can talk," she said.

And the tree replied, "Yes! I can talk. I don't talk to people because no one sees me or even recognizes that I'm there. I am very lonely, so I have no friends."

Emily said, "I can be your friend or maybe even best friends."

The tree was so happy that he found a friend.

It was time for Emily and her father to accept or deny the house. Of course they kept the house because Emily pleaded and put on her puppy face to persuade her father and it worked. So Emily and her father headed home to get some papers to get the house today. While they were driving, Emily could not stop talking to her father on how the tree talked to her. Her dad did not believe her, but Emily knew she was not going crazy. Emily's father explained to Emily that they can't have the tree by the pool.

"Why?" Emily asked.

Emily's father explained that if it is super windy outside and she is in the pool and the tree falls, it can hurt her.

"I would be so sad because maybe you will get hurt badly."

Emily said to her father that she understands but she doesn't want it to come down. All the way home, that's all they talked about. When they reached home, they grabbed the papers on the table and left immediately because the lady was waiting for a long time. So the lady signed the paper, and then they got her the money and got the house.

As soon as they moved in, Emily's father decided to start cleaning the house by calling the gardeners to come cut the grass and remove the tree. The gardeners finally came and cut the grass and added some roses, plants, and other flowers to the backyard. Then it was time for them to cut down the tree, but they couldn't cut it down because Emily was sitting on it. So the gardeners called her dad. Emily decided to climb the tree so they won't cut it down. Her dad asked her to come down several times, but she refused.

"The tree has to go," her dad said.

But Emily will not listen. She climbed higher comforting the tree. Emily cried and cried and then gave the tree a big hug and told him sorry and she loves him. The tree was sad that he had to die but also happy he was able to find a friend. When Emily came down the tree, her father noticed that she was really sad and that she looked so unhappy when talking to the tree. So he decided to pay the gardeners for the job they already did and told them thank you. Emily was so happy that her father let her keep the tree. Until this day, Emily is twelve years old, and she still sits in her backyard under the tree. She and her father trim it every day and give it the amount of water it needs. After this, the tree felt so happy that he finally found a friend who loves him and never leaves him. The tree was lonely but now saved by Emily.

Now to him who is able to do immeasurably more than all
we ask or imagine, according to his power that is at work
within us, to him be glory in the church and in Christ Jesus
throughout all generations, for ever and ever! Amen.

—Ephesians 3:20–21

October 18, 2019

Dear Daddy,

You promised that you would do things opposite to your father—and you did not; you still walked way. You promised that you will always be with me. Where are you when I need you the most? Dad, when you were home, it was as if we were in our own little heaven. I felt secure and safe as if you swept us away to a petite, out-layer town—to a realm of safety, orderliness, and refuge.

I just wonder how hard it must have been for you as a child growing up without your parents always being there. It must have been difficult for you. Why do you want me to experience the same thing? How can you see your child grow without a parent and not hurt and run to them? Daddy, I dream of the day that we will be reunited; we can get up and lie in bed and worship together, or after worship and breakfast, have our early morning movies still in PJs cuddled with Mommy on her bed. Those little things mean so much, especially when you had it and it is all gone. As a child, you long for it; you have hopes that it will happen again.

I know it is difficult for anyone to give something that they do not have; that's why I forgive you for leaving me. You have not experienced the powerful love between a parent and a child, so you cannot give me that. You do not know what it means to sacrifice everything thing for a child because no one in your life was so unselfish to sacrifice all for you. However, I am thankful that God gave me such a special type of mommy, one who always does everything for me with love and never complains and who always places my needs above her own.

Dad, I was drowning, and Jesus helped me to emerge from the hurt that you inflicted on me. It was preaching and singing that saved me when you checked yourself out of my life. Through music and the spoken Word, God revealed Himself to me and assured me that He will be my daddy. I know that you believe visiting us every couple of months was you being there, but mentally I knew that my daddy was gone. Please give your heart to Jesus, Daddy—all of it. He wants all of your heart. I would like you to be saved in God's kingdom, so if your salvation means being away from me, I understand.

Love you, Daddy,
Chae

Yours, Lord, is the greatness and the power
and the glory and the majesty and the splendor,
for everything in heaven and earth is yours.
Yours, Lord, is the kingdom;
you are exalted as head overall.

—1 Chronicles 29:11

November 18, 2019

Dear Daddy,

Despite my hurt, I want you to know that you are appreciated. I now grasp the true gravity and extent of your presence now that you are not here; the absence is abhorring. You may not have been as verbal as Mummy, and you may never have been the parent who shepherded me from place to place on activities or even the primary parent I called in times of anguish. But I've recognized that your disposition, your inspiration, your personality, and your silent yet resilient demeanor are priceless to me.

In Mommy's fury, you remain unruffled, well put together, unyielding, and kind. And though I naturally tend to be disposed more in the direction of my mother's bothersome strong-willed nature, I am privileged to have garnered a few drops of your calm charisma laced into my personality.

Daddy, it is not always bad with you; although on and off a couple months here and a couple months there, you've instilled fairness, humbleness, kindness, and independence in me. As those characters grow, I want you there to prune the leaves of my behavior so that I can flourish into a beautiful tree. In you, I see the gift of love and always being ready to give. Your desire to attain greatness is impeccable, and I applaud you for that. Every day I endeavor to replicate your ostensibly effortless commitment to self-love and high level of personal care. I must add that you have been very far from perfect, but I've seen you develop and become an enhanced form of yourself, which makes me delighted. But it has also given me hope in you and faith in Christ that one day you will be with me again. Knowing that God is reclaiming your life and you are acknowledging your need of Him gives me hope.

Daddy, you are the measuring rod from which I will determine the enormity of a man. You are the example that I will be looking at, so please show me that with Jesus, people have the power to change and become someone incredible though the whole world may think that they are not.

You are loved,
Your beloved Chae

Be strong and courageous. Do not be afraid or terrified
because of them, for the Lord you God goes with
you: He will never leave you nor forsake you.

—Deuteronomy 31:6

December 18, 2019

Dear Dad,

I always knew you to be compassionate, thoughtful, caring, and encouraging. What happened to you? It seems for the past couple years, you are struggling maintaining those characters. Please allow Jesus in your life to give you the strength to cultivate those great characters. When the enemy takes hold of a person's life, they are transformed into another being. And I know you cannot see because the enemy has blinded you and have you wrapped up and tangled up in him, but I want to assure you that I am praying for your release from the enemy.

I knew you to be easygoing and kindhearted. I knew you to be a truth seeker of sorts, a deep thinker, and an independent thinker. I knew you to be someone who would challenge nonsense. That's not who I see when I see you, Daddy. I am crying out to God for your soul. I will not and cannot allow the enemy to take my daddy. You are my great daddy, and I am praying for you.

With the most abundant love as the world can control,
Your daughter, Chae

So do not fear, for I am with you; do not be dismayed,
for I am your God. I will strengthen you and help you;
   I will uphold you with my righteous right hand.

—Isaiah 41:10

January 18, 2020

Dear Daddy,

Even when you are not with me, your presence will constantly be in our home. I can feel you when we sit at the table, eating your favorite meal. I sometimes hear your voice in the midnight when I can't sleep and you would play scrabble with me until I feel tired. I feel you all around me. When I go on the basketball court, I am hoping you were there to play with me. I know you are invisibly a part of everything that I do, but is it too much to ask for having you around me all the time? I feel your love enclose me with every gasp of breath I take. Probably it is because I have never been so connected to another person as I am with you. But don't worry too much; I am getting better missing you. I cry less and pray more.

Daddy! You will always be my best friend and my greatest supporter. Your continual certainty in my boundless potential gives me hope every single day. Daddy! My love for you is infinite. I just wish I can have more time with you because together we have the power.

Daddy! I give you my word—I will confidently pursue my wildest dreams. However, I know that with you, I can accomplish much more because you motivate me to reach my goals. I know that Jesus has the power to make me achieve greatness, but I do want my earthly father to help push me. I will always work hard as you and Mom taught me to and never give up or hold back. I will try my best to do the right things and always for the right reasons.

Daddy! I am really honored to be your daughter—the center of your world. But can you please come home?

Love always,
Chae

Have I not commanded you? Be strong and courageous.
Do not be terrified; do not be discouraged, for the
LORD your God will be with you wherever you go.

—Joshua 1:9

But the Lord stood at my side and gave me strength, so that through me the message might be fully proclaimed and all the Gentiles might hear it. And I was delivered from the lion's mouth.

—2 Timothy 4:17

February 18, 2020

Dear Dad,

Remember that time that I got so angry and I did not want to talk to you for a day? I told Mommy that I do not want to talk to you, and you told her, "Just give the child the phone." When I got on, you took everything as a joke. You were just laughing and said, "Child, you are too much, but I love you to the moon and back." I must have been eleven. That year, I was angry with you for not coming up. You stayed away so long I thought you had forgotten me. When you eventually call with all your excuses, I did not want to listen, but Mommy made me talk to you.

You should be grateful for Mommy because if it was my child, I would not let her talk to you. It was terrible what you did, taking so long to call me. You were so full of it I had so many horrible feelings you couldn't even know. But thank God for His love in me. I thank God every day; if it was not for the love of God in me, no matter how much my heart ached for you, I would not have spoken to you ever again. When Mommy said that you were on the phone, I was not phased. There were so many questions in my head, and I know you would not answer.

But when you think of it, you and I are exactly the same. I know it's hard for me to see myself in the body of my father. But every day my mom reminds me that we are alike. Every day she says in her creole, "C'enfant papa." I am sure a smaller, girlier, and stubborn version of your ways. Mom says we have OCD, and that I know I inherited from you. My room has to be lined up, everything in its places; even my hangers need to have the same numbers of inches apart. However, that is as far it goes with being like you. I am not going to make the same mindless decisions you made at the age I am now. My mom has already cursed all inherent bad habits from me, and I stand on God's word that I will be a representative of Him when and whenever I go.

Therefore I will fall but I will rise. I will make mistakes but not wallow in them and rather rise above them. Daddy, just as God has created me to glorify Him in my body, my thoughts, and my deeds,

He made you just the same. It is just a matter of choice. Will you choose to allow Jesus to recreate you into what you were supposed to be? Daddy, it is time for you to run to Jesus. We do not have a lot of time, so run to him now. Leave all the pleasures of the world behind and run to him. Maybe sooner rather than later, I will grow up and face challenges; but I want to continue to remind myself with God, all things are possible. Stay strong, Daddy. God has a plan for your life.

Love,
Forever your dearest daughter, Chae

Finally, be strong in the Lord and in His mighty power.

—Ephesians 6:10

March 18, 2020

Dear Daddy,

For loading us up in the van with absolutely no endpoint in mind, yet we began our journey, shows how fun and adventurous you were. I need you to be that person again. I need my fun-loving daddy back. I believe that he is somewhere inside you. I am praying every day that my daddy resurface inside of you—the daddy that likes taking risk because it is exciting and carefree and because you knew it made me happy. Daddy, you are so courageous when Mommy is scared to try something. You just go ahead and do it, and many times, you were correct. I miss that. Mommy is always the one spotting a trouble. But many times, your bravery of taking the risk not only made us successful; but above all, we were able to explore the unknown. I need my carefree, fun-loving daddy back. Where are you?

Love you, Dad,
Chae

I am strong in the Lord and in the power of His might.

—Ephesians 6:10

April 18, 2020

Dear Dad,

About three years ago, my mom and I, we were driving through the Arizona desert. It was hot and scary, and we were practically the only vehicle on the road for hours. The mountains were steep, and the land was so bare there was nothing really in sight. As we cruise along the desert, all I can think about is my daddy. If only you were there, I would not be scared. Probably we would be singing and laughing. Nightfall came, and it grew even more fearful as we were driving around hunting for a hotel to spend the night. The very exciting new trip across the coastline, fulfilling our amazing travel dreams, provided me with that unforgettable horrific experience. This memory is heavily entrenched within our hearts, not as an awesome memorable experience that we hoped it to be but one of fear and sadness—the sadness of being alone, being without you. Oh, how I wish you were there, Daddy.

I can still remember entering that hotel. It was not the best hotel that I have ever been to; but it was the most gratifying hotel of my life because I was tired, scared, and hungry and was so happy we found a hotel to rest the night. My mom did everything to cheer me up, but there was nothing that she could have done to replace that despondency of not having you around and to fill that void that I felt in the very pit of my stomach. Whenever we did something fun, I could always imagine you being there, and the thing that should bring joy to me now brought pain and anger because I cannot enjoy it without you.

I still forgive you, Daddy, for leaving because now I am older, I understand that when you do not have Jesus, the devil controls your life. The Bible says that even when we try to do good, we do bad, and it is not because we are bad people. It is simply because of the power the enemy has over us. When I was too young to speak, you were such a great dad. I remember you combing my hair when Mommy was out of town. I remember us dancing to non-Christian music. Mom would catch us, and she would say, "Please do not bring the devil in this house." And we would just chuckle our heart out. I miss you being the exciting person in our family. Mommy is too serious sometimes. I am grateful that I have a daddy even if I do not see you all the time. I just want more time with you, Daddy.

I will soon grow up to be a teenager and then an adult, and I will not have the opportunity to enjoy all those childish things with you. Remember when you would carry me on your shoulders, oil me down with Vaseline because I had eczema, yet telling me that I was the most beautiful girl in the whole wide world. Despite all the hurt I feel for you not being here, those words made me feel incredibly beautiful, and no one can tell me otherwise. Thank you, Daddy, for answering our phone call when we needed you the most even if it was not all the time.

Do you remember when you chanted the *Da-Da* song for five minutes and I couldn't stop laughing? It was funny then, but now I see I still walk through life with that same amount of joy. Daddy, thank you for the reminder of how special I am.

Your baby girl,
Chae

In quietness and confidence shall be my strength.

—Isaiah 30:15

May 18, 2020

My dearest daddy,

It is such a joy when you come to visit me. I wish you did not have to visit and just stay home. I love spending time with you and doing things with you. You are my hero; I idolize you. You may not know that, but even my signature is shaped just like yours. I want to emulate all the great parts of you.

I am not sure if you know, but I am always carrying so much baggage of hurt because of you. Sadly, I regularly let it out on Mommy; as teenage girls, we almost certainly do that with our mommies. I am trying my best to own up to it and do better. I have made peace with the fact that you choose to live in another place, but I will not give up on you.

When I tell people that you left me, I can tell that they feel sad for me. However, I am not sad for me because I got to meet the best daddy in the world a little better. I am happy that you were a nice, fun-loving daddy to me once it lasted. To me, when you were around, my world was perfect; and when you left, my world was shattered. But Jesus showed me that no human being should shatter my world because He created my world and has the power to keep me in check even if I get in sticky situations. Even when you and mommy yelled and screamed at each other, I knew that you loved me, but I am not sure now. You were the one who taught me how to get on my mom's good side when I did something wrong. I learn that from you. You taught me how to say I am sorry and how to be humble. So it was not all sadness for me; there were some good times, right, Daddy? I would give it all to have you back home. But praise to Daddy Jesus. He always has my back; He is always with me.

When people ask about you and how I feel that you are not with me, most times family, I tell them all the time how you come to me in dreams and come alive in the stories I write at school. Before it was painful to talk about, but now I just say that I don't know if I ever felt like I lost my Father, referring to Daddy Jesus. My relationship with my Daddy upstairs is constantly evolving all the time, and as I get closer to Him, the less I feel the need to cry for you. You tore my heart, Daddy. It is very sad that the first guy to break my heart is my own daddy, but the enemy will not make me hate you. I just feel pity for you that you missed out on a wonderful relationship with me—and do not blame it on Mommy this time. You did it all by yourself. However, every day as I get to know my other daddy, I love Him more; and I love you more. Daddy Jesus never makes me cry, and the more I fall in love with Him, the more I love you. You should get to know Him. He wants to be your daddy too, and He can really teach you some new and amazing tricks on how to be the best daddy.

I love you. Always,
Chae

God gives power to the weak. And to those who
have no might, He increases strength

—Isaiah 40:29

June 18, 2020

Dear Daddy,

My mom told me today that you will be coming for my graduation. I said that was great, but I was lying. I knew that you were not going to come. You have put every store, every bus, and every God knows what in front of us; so I just wanted her to think that I was happy. The truth is I really do not want you to come.

Daddy, you do what makes you happy, and so I want what makes me happy. Do you know what makes me happy? My mommy. So I do not want you to come home to make her sad. So stay where you are until God has changed you completely, and then you can come home to us. In the meanwhile, we are praying for you that God works miraculously with you. I have learned over the past couple years that the only person I can rely on is Daddy Jesus. He can do the impossible, and he knows what is best for me.

We will keep you prayed up,
Chae

When you pass through the waters,
I will be with you;
and when you pass through the rivers,
they will not sweep over you.
When you walk through the fire,
you will not be burned;
the flames will not set you ablaze.

—Isaiah 43:2

July 18, 2020

Hey, Dad,

Do you remember me? It's your daughter? We don't necessarily have the emblematic father-daughter relationship, and it is because you have never really been around long enough to get to know me, not as a babbling baby but this amazing free-spirited teen with a strong personality. You've never really tried and developed anything with me, and I bet you do not have any real, authentic memories of me after the age of seven. You have never helped me do my homework or read to me before bed at least after age seven. You were not even around when I got baptized which is one of the greatest milestones in my life.

Even to this this day, I think about the wonderful relationship we could have had if you had just chosen to be unselfish. When have you been unselfish dad? Wasn't I more important? You could have left what you were doing and be with me when I needed you the most; that's what daddies do. If you cared, you could have went to my teacher-parent conferences to learn more about my academic needs, goals, and strengths. If you cared enough, you would have chosen to be with me to our family dinners when I was a much younger child instead of my uncles. If we had that important, special relationship that every girl desire from their daddy, you could be sitting in the audience and praising God with me every time I preach; but sadly you weren't there.

It was absolutely my mom who raised me into the teenager I am today. She did it all on her own, Daddy. Where were you, Daddy? She tolerated my gibberish while dealing with her own nonsense that you inflicted on her. Every morning, she woke up at six, sometimes five; made me breakfast; got me prepared; and then took me to school. That is part of a daddy's job, right, and you failed. She also had to rush home from school, pick me up and take me home, prepare dinner, help me with homework, spend time with me, worship with me, and then put me to bed.

My mom was the only one ever to be at school occasions, humbly smiling at my accomplishments. Where were you? There were many times I did not have all what I wanted, but she always ensured I had what I needed. She has bent over backward to give me what I need and more, and all you have done practically my whole life is cause me pain and tears. For the past ten years, I have spent Mother's Day and of course Father's Day with my mommy. When I was younger, I would be upset that I couldn't be with the guy who helped put me in existence, but now I really just think of my mom as my dad.

My entire life, I would reprove myself for you not being with us. I felt I would come up with reasons for why you didn't love me enough. At some point in time, I persuaded myself I did not deserve a daddy and I was not worthy enough to have a great dad like all my other friends at school. I soon got stressed out when my friend's daddy came to pick them up from school—so stressed out that I got angry. When my mom came to pick me up from school, I would be angry with her for no apparent reason. I remember one day when my mom picked me up, I just snapped at her, and she cried because she understood my frustration. Then she hugged me, and we cried as I share with her my sadness. I still remember that day like it was yesterday. What made my mommy so special and empathetic is when I cried especially for my dad, she cried with me so I knew that she understood my pain.

Praise be to the God and Father of our Lord Jesus Christ, the Father of compassion and the God of all comfort, who comforts us in all our troubles, so that we can comfort those in any trouble with the comfort we ourselves receive from God.

—2 Corinthians 1:3–4

August 18, 2020

Dear Daddy,

    Today is my birthday, and as usual, you are not here again. It is as if I do not have a daddy. My mom wants to throw me a birthday party, but what is the point. Even if my cousins, friends, and Grandma come, there is no daddy. I do not feel like celebrating without my daddy. I think I will just go to the mall and allow the day to pass quickly.

Chae

Come to me, all you who are weary and
burdened, and I will give you rest.

—Matthew 11:28

September 18, 2020

Dear Daddy,

Today was tough for me. School is about to begin, and we are not sure if we will be in a class which is great in one way because we will be at home. But on the other hand, I will miss my friends and the teachers. Although I will see them online, it is not the same. Being quarantined has its advantages, but socially the disadvantages far outweighs the advantages. However, I will not complain. Many people are dead because of the corona, and God has spared me and my family. Although I miss you, I want you to be safe. Flying on a plane right now is taking an unnecessary risk, so it is better that you are safe.

I was so happy when I saw you on WhatsApp yesterday you have no idea. However, it made me miss you more, seeing your face and hoping that you were quarantined with us. I definitely will not be that bored because you are so much fun, Daddy. I pray that the corona crisis will be all over soon and you can find your way back to me. I will not stop praying for you, Daddy. I know that you are way better than what the devil throws at you. You are so much better than what the world sees. One day, God is going to reveal the real person you are, and then the world will know that God is powerful. Do not stop wrestling with God, Daddy. He wants to save you. I get mad at times, but I know who I believe in. Jesus will make a difference; He will make all things new.

With love,
Chae

Be strong and take heart,
all you who hope in the Lord.

—Psalm 31:24

November 18, 2020

Dear Daddy,

I thought you would always be with me. As a little girl, I never imagine that you wouldn't be with me all the time. I always believed that my daddy who would always play basketball with me just before bed would always be with me. But I guess I was sadly mistaken. I always believed that my fun-loving and nurturing daddy would always kiss me before I go to bed for a long time; then again I was sadly mistaken.

The misconception I had that this caring and thoughtful person I call daddy would always be with me was soon realized. Don't worry, Daddy. Most times, I do not blame you but the devil. He took my daddy from me, and I know that Jesus can bring him back. That warm-hearted and soft person who took me to the store when buying a car or, when shopping for clothes, asks my opinion on what he should buy would not just disappear on me. There are absolutely no words to describe the immense hurt and pain. When I feel sad, I ask God for the strength to hold on. I believe that my Jesus has made me strong. He is preparing me for something much more painful, and I will bear it because I was able to overcome the pain of losing my daddy.

The power and love of God has seen me through many, many dark days. My way of dealing with all the anguish is resting my case in the arms of Jesus. When I have cried and I have prayed, I dry my tears, get up from my knees, and move forward. I cannot thank God enough for the courage that I have gained during this experience. Christ will forever be my strong tower of strength. I know that I have a long way to go, but my courage shows an amazing example of true Christian persecution and the audacity of hope.

I'm extremely thankful that God gives courage!

Love,
Chae

I have told you these things, so that in me you may
have peace. In this world you will have trouble.
But take heart! I have overcome the world.

—John 16:33

December 18, 2020

Dear Dad,

I hope you know how sad I feel today. Christmas is seven days away, and all I can think about is if you are going to come home this Christmas. I would be super excited if you do, but I have learned to never get my hopes up because you never know what can happen. There are no words written on this page that can accurately express the fondness I feel for you and the bountiful joy that I will experience if you are home for Christmas. Many little girls wait for Santa for Christmas to get their favorite toys, but I wait for my daddy. I would give up a million dollars to have you as my Christmas gift.

Daddy! You are the best gift that any little girl wants for Christmas, wrapped in the power of love. Your love to me is worth more than any material thing that I may receive for Christmas. Material things are used and thrown away. They are eaten; they are placed as a monument in our home. But your love lasts a lifetime—it resonates for eternity. That's why you are the best Christmas gift. Whenever you hugged me with your strong arms of love and gave me your tightest and warmest embrace, you made me feel so special. In Jesus's arms, there is more safety and assurance. That's why I know that I do not need anything else but Him to protect me. It is so amazing to be cuddled in the arms of both my heavenly and earthly daddy. In those arms, I feel refuge; I gain strength. Please, Daddy, do not take your arms from around me. Hold on, and if you feel like letting go, ask Jesus for the power to grip on because I feel like you are slipping away.

I love you, Daddy!
Chae

"For I know the plans I have for you," says the Lord. "They are plans for good and not for disaster, to give you a future and a hope."

—Jeremiah 29:11

January 18, 2021

Dear Dad,

I will always cherish our incalculable father-daughter recollections for a lifetime. I am elated for all those special memories that we shared, and that's what keeps me going at times when I want to break down and cry. Cry for fear that I will not see you again. Cry for fear that eternity will be lost to you forever if you do not strip yourself of this world and have Christ enter into you.

Though I am thankful that you have started down the road to safety with Jesus—you are reading your Bible and are more intentional about your relationship with him—I sometimes get scared that if you do not stay on the path, it may be too late for you. Daddy! Every minute that you are alive, please spend it with God. Make your moments with Jesus be an unforgettable experience. Ones that will constantly be on your mind. Ones you can meditate on day and night, minute by minute. Let the moments with Jesus be embedded within your hearts so your thoughts are always on Him. I want you to be saved, Daddy, and if it means not being without us, then Jesus knows what's best.

I love you, Daddy, and please choose Jesus,
Chae

When doubts filled my mind, your comfort
gave me renewed hope and cheer.

—Psalm 94:19

February 18, 2021

Dear Daddy,

There is no need to project a tough emotionless exterior. I know that you cry when you are sad and upset; I see you broken when things get tough. Jesus also sees you, and He knows that you need him. He is listening right now. Please tell him your aches and pains and where it hurts; He will lessen the pain. Jesus knows that you need Him, and He needs you to do a special job for Him. I need you desperately too, Daddy. I am experiencing some huge changes in my life, and I need you to help me maneuver those challenges.

As a little girl, the excitement of you coming home unexpected and showing up at my school or church has worn off. I want you to be front and center in my life now. I am thirteen. Mr. Hormones are raising its ugly head my way, and I need you to protect me and help me tackle him. Mom cannot do it alone. Most of the time, she does not get me—not like you do. I am at that age where my mommy is my greatest fan, my greatest love, yet she has no idea the volcanic eruptions that happen in my head and body; and I feel that you would know what to say to me to help me through it. Mommy was always the one that only sees black and white. You see colors, and that variety would add some flexibility to my stress levels.

Dad, I want you to know that no one in the world will love you like your little Chris, and you mean all the world to me. You tell me every day that you want me to be a nun, and at first, I had no idea why you would say that to me. But now I understand you are scared that I will get a boyfriend. But you do not have to worry about that. Remember he has to go through Mommy, and if I were a guy, I would rather be single than go through Mommy. Then again, do not be scared for me; just be there for me and pray that Jesus orders my steps.

Love you!

Therefore my heart is glad, and my glory rejoices; my flesh also will rest in hope.

—Psalm 16:9

March 18, 2021

Dearest Dad,

The pain of missing you is one of the worst thing that I have ever faced. I just cannot imagine feeling anything worse. It is exceptionally painful because I do not know when I will see you again. With this virus, who knows what will happen. The feeling of you walking out on me is similar to bereavement. I know it may seem that you see me every couple months, but it is not enough. I will not accept that is all you can do. There is so much greatness inside of you; only Daddy Jesus can allow you to see that if you let him. It has been rough. I am not going to lie. But I get up every day hoping that today is going to be a better day.

Even when I know that you do not want to be with me, I ask God to give me the courage to hope that you want to be with me. Within my fear, pain, and grief, I ask God each day to give me the strength to believe that everything is going to be okay. Christ then gives me the strength to extend the quality of my mind and spirit which enables me to face my difficulties.

I thank Daddy Jesus for the courage He permits me to have as I face the extreme hurt and pain of losing you—the courage with gallant and dauntless boldness to face my internal battle and depend on Him. Not having a parent at any stage in your life is horrible, particularly during that puberty stage. That stress-prone stage is when I need you the most, Daddy, and you are not there. The changes in my mood, thinking, and level of anxiety causes stress; and you have brought on a whole new level of stress by not being there. As my body reacts to the demand for my daddy and you are not there, it makes me feel really like nobody, and the stress level naturally brought on my puberty is now amplified. You say you love me? Then prove it. Come home.

Love,
Chae

Praise be to the God and Father of our Lord Jesus Christ, the
Father of compassion and the God of all comfort, who comforts
us in all our troubles, so that we can comfort those in any
trouble with the comfort we ourselves receive from God.

—2 Corinthians 1:3–4

June 20, 2021

Happy Father's Day, Mommy!

Dear Daddy,

It is Father's Day, and do you know why am I saying Happy Father's Day to my mommy? Because she has been my dad for the last couple years. I think we should celebrate mommies on Father's Day because they have fulfilled the role of a dad and a mom. Or why not call it Super Mommy Day instead. My mommy gives the extra love because she wanted me to know that I am loved. She wants me to understand that you left because you felt insecure and unloved yourself, not that I should feel that way. She was patient every time I cried, when I ask her to leave my room because she understood the pain that I felt. She hugged me when I got upset sometimes for absolutely no reason.

She was kind to me when I ask her to leave me alone. Because you made me so sad, all I wanted to do was be alone. She made me meals three times a day with love and treated me triple times as a princess. She lied for you to make me feel you cared. She deserves a medal. That's why today is Super Mommy Day, and she is my father.

No offense, Daddy. You called sporadically. You send me money occasionally. You spoke to me infrequently. But my mom—Lord bless her—is at every basketball game, gymnastics, and piano lessons. Where were you? She is my super mommy. Happy Father's Day, Mommy! Don't be upset, Daddy. You know she deserves it.

Love,
Chae

July 18, 2021

Dear Dad,

Today my teacher asked us to write an essay beginning with "After the rain stopped, I walked outside," and all I could think about is you. So this is what I came up with.

The Essence of Hope

After the rain stopped, I walked outside. Houses were destroyed, trees were bent, and parents were crying on their knees, wondering if their children would ever come home. This hurricane was known as mere devastation because it brought agony to families, as well as mine. I walked all over New York City trying to find my dad. I was calling my dad's name, "Daddy, Daddy, Daddy, where are you?" hoping that he did not die from this hurricane. My dad was working at New York City Skyscraper Academy, and today he was supposed to be working on a new skyscraper. Oh—not that thought. Maybe I shouldn't be thinking that way, but what if my dad was on the top of the skyscraper fixing it when the hurricane showed up? So I continued to look for him in desperation until I came across the police station. I looked inside to see if anyone could help me, but then I saw dead police officers on the floor. I was so horrified because all of them were dead and they can't help me find my father. I cried and I cried asking Jesus who will help me find my father.

I walked back home with my head in my hand not knowing what to say to my mother. When I reached home, I told my mom I don't know where he is and no one could help because they all died. My mom cried knowing she will not see her husband again. I told my mom I will do everything in my power to find him dead or alive.

My mom said to me, "Just give up. Give up, Georgia. Maybe he's dead."

I looked into my mom's eyes with hope that I will find my father. I said to my mom that Robert Fulghum declared that anyone's imagination is stronger than knowledge, that myth is more potent than history, that dreams are more powerful than facts, that hope always triumphs over experience, and that laughter is the only cure for grief. And I believe that love is stronger than death. My mom put her hands on the side of my head and told me to "go. Go and find your father, and one day, you will become a stronger hopeful leader."

My mom told me, "I will see you on the news someday and might as well hear your name be called, 'as the president of the United States of America declaring to the American citizens to have hope and never give up.'"

I left the house, roaming around the streets, looking around, and asking every house if they saw my dad. I even showed pictures of him, but they still said they never saw him. I went to this last house in confidence and hope that this person can help find my father, and yes, he did. He told me, he saw my dad walking to the academy at five o'clock that morning, but never walked back. The guy said that he greeted my dad every morning and evening when he pass on his street. Then he started to talk about how my dad was so kind, and how he helped him fix his car. "When did he fix your car?" I asked him.

He said, "Oh I forgot to tell you, he helped me fix it today, then he told me he was going to the best mechanic in New Jersey." The man said.

I was so excited to hear such great news, because I thought my dad was on the skyscraper when it fell. Immediately, I ran home to give my mom the good news.

"Mom!" I yelled from across the street. I was so overjoyed that someone had seen my dad. I could not wait to get to the house. When my mom heard the news, she was so elated that she burst out crying. Everyone thought he was dead after his skyscraper fell, but now it appeared that he was not the person on the skyscraper. The man who saw my dad gave us a flicker of hope.

"Just breathe," I told my mom, who was trying to catch her breath—still shocked by the news.

My mother and I decided to look down every street in New York City to check again if my father wasn't here before we went to New Jersey. We looked and looked, but he wasn't there. So we decided to go to New Jersey. Luckily the highway wasn't damaged and the cleaners were removing the trees and branches from the street. On our way to New Jersey, we encountered an enormous tree right in front of the exit. I was so upset because I wanted to know if my dad was okay. My mom called a tree removal company and told them to remove the tree so we could pass through because it was an emergency. They told her that she had to wait until the next day, because many of the workers had died in the storm and they did not have enough manpower. My mom agreed to wait, but in her voice you could hear the sound or frustration. My mom "took matters in her own hand' and attempted to move the debris in the road. Of course the tree did not budge.

"Are you crazy?" I yelled at my mom. "You will hurt yourself." She then ordered me to call my uncles to come and help us move the tree in the road. My uncles tied the tree to their car and moved it. Sooner than we thought, we were on our way to find my dad.

Be strong and courageous. Do not fear or be in dread
of them, for it is the Lord your God who goes with
you. He will not leave you or forsake you

—Deuteronomy 31:6

ABOUT THE AUTHOR

Christy-ana Williams-Rutil is a high school student at the Berea SDA Academy who loves to sing and preach God's Word. She has a passion to pursue high academic standards and to learn lifelong skills to make a positive impact in her community. She is the daughter of Dr. Laura Williams and Wallace Rutil. She is a pathfinder and a member of Real Truth SDA Church in Framingham, Massachusetts. She is a member of the New England North Personal Ministries Federation. She has volunteered in the community services team at Berea Church, helping to serve food to the Roxbury and Dorchester neighborhood area. Her hobbies include public speaking, vocal music, piano, gymnastics, basketball, track and field, and flag football.